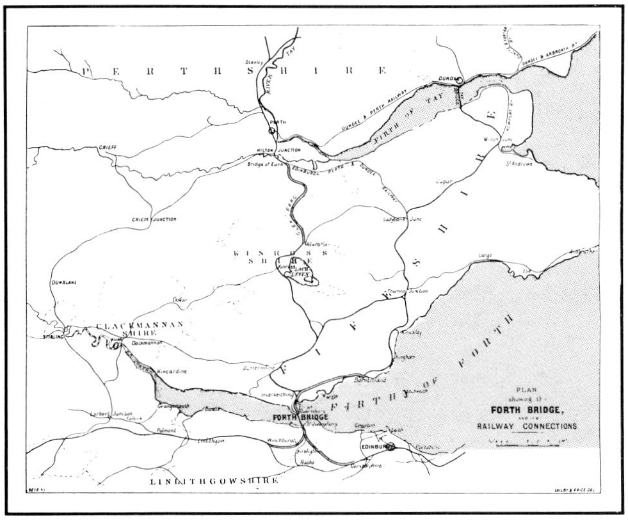

BRIDGE ACROSS THE CENTURY

The story of the Forth Railway Bridge sounds like a romantic chapter from a fairy tale of science, but its purpose is intensely practical . . .

Benjamin Baker

A Victorian gentleman who wished to confirm his belief in Progress had only to climb aboard a railway train. By the 1880s the East Coast line cut an audacious swathe through the country—from Dover via London, York and Newcastle to Edinburgh—the great engineers harnessing imagination and invention to overcome each obstacle in their way with a bridge or a tunnel, a cutting or an embankment.

"The Engineers, with their gigantic works, sweep everything before them in this Victorian era", was how the Forth Bridge's designer, Benjamin Baker, put it. But a few miles beyond Edinburgh, this triumphant procession over natural forces came to an abrupt halt.

When the sound of steam died away at Queensferry, the only thing to be heard was the gentle lapping of water on the shores of the Firth of Forth. The railway lines through Fife to the north lay a mile away over the treacherous currents of the Forth estuary. Nature was issuing one last, mighty challenge to Progress—and one of which others were waiting to take advantage.

Realising the obstacles presented by the Firth of Forth and, to a lesser extent, the Firth of Tay, the wily West Coast railway barons were threatening to cut across the country with new railway lines to steal the entire Northern and North Eastern railway custom of Scotland.

Their plan was to be rudely interrupted, however, by the timely intervention of a more ambitious plan by far: to build the colossal bridge across the Forth which would ultimately prevent the construction of many miles of railway to the west and extend the East Coast line initially as far north as Aberdeen.

And so it was that thousands of men descended on the peaceful villages of North and South Queensferry and laboured day and night (Sundays excluded) for seven years to build the longest bridge in the world—and the greatest monument to engineering and industrial skills of its era ■

PRELUDE: FROM DREAMS TO DISASTER

For centuries monarchs, pilgrims, warriors and ordinary folk must have longed for an alternative to the risk of sudden drenching, seasickness and even terror inherent in crossing the temperamental Queensferry Passage by ferryboat. It was not until the end of the 19th century that the seemingly impossible dream of bridging the Forth became a reality, and, as the Tay Bridge Disaster demonstrated, such a momentous achievement was hardly possible only a decade earlier.

Throughout that century plans to bridge the Forth estuary at the point known as the Queensferry Passage had been discussed and abandoned. The success of the Rotherhithe Tunnel under the River Thames even led to surveys for a Forth Tunnel. But that idea was dropped by 1806 and, 12 years later, James Anderson, a civil engineer in Edinburgh, drew up plans for a bridge of chains. These plans, too, came to nothing—fortunately; for, as a Forth Bridge engineer commented later in the century, Anderson's bridge "was so light a structure that it would hardly have been visible on a dull day, and after a heavy gale, it would no longer be seen on a clear day either".

In 1849 the Edinburgh and Northern Railway changed its name to the Edinburgh, Perth and Dundee Railway and recruited the young Thomas Bouch as its engineer. Bouch became obsessed by the problems of crossing the Forth and Tay estuaries and devised a means of running railway goods wagons on to the steam ferries. Though his idea was not entirely original, the "floating railways" with which Bouch's name was associated became a wonder of the age.

He was a force to be reckoned with in the era of Railwaymania and, when he put his plans to bridge the two estuaries to the directors of the North British Railway Company, they took him seriously.

By 1860 the company had fixed on a site between Blackness Castle and Charleston on the north shore of the Forth, and an Act of Parliament authorised the construction of a Forth bridge in 1865. Preliminary work revealed that the bed of the Forth was loose and unpredictable at that point—a fact which, aggravated by the complexities surrounding the reorganisation of the North British Railway Company the following year, led to Bouch's first plan being abandoned. It was not until 1873 that the Forth Bridge Company was formed to construct, to Thomas Bouch's design, a suspension bridge on the site of the present bridge.

Bouch's 20-year-old dream of bridging the Forth and Tay estuaries had begun to assume reality in July, 1871, when the foundation stone of the Tay Bridge was laid.

In the last days of the decade, the Bouch family, ensconced in the comfort of their home in Edinburgh's West End, had more reason to count their blessings than to worry about the storm roaring down Scotland's east coast.

It was four days after Christmas: the Tay Bridge had been in operation for 19 months and Thomas Bouch had his knighthood; Margaret Bouch had laid the foundation stone for the Forth Bridge in 1873; their engineer son was supervising his father's designs for the bridge over the South Esk at Montrose. Work had begun on the Forth Bridge which was to be the head of the household's ultimate achievement. Together, the three bridges would complete the long-dreamed-of route to the North, from Edinburgh to Dundee and Aberdeen, carrying the trains of the Great Northern, the North Eastern, the Midland and the North British railway companies over the deep-sea inlet barriers of the east coast.

At this zenith of his achievement, Sir Thomas little expected the blow from which he would never recover. On the night of December 28, 1879, a telegram arrived at his home:

> TERRIBLE ACCIDENT ON BRIDGE ONE OR MORE OF HIGH GIRDERS BLOWN DOWN AM NOT SURE OF THE SAFETY OF THE LAST DOWN EDINBR TRAIN WILL ADVISE FURTHER AS SOON AS CAN BE OBTAINED

By the cruel light of that dawn, the extent of the disaster was all too evident. The Tay Bridge had crumbled into the estuary, sweeping the Edinburgh train and an estimated 75 passengers to their deaths with the debris of brick and metal.

Work on the Forth Bridge was stopped by a formal Abandonment Act speedily passed by Parliament, and subsequent investigations into the Tay Bridge shook public confidence in Bouch, both the man and his assumed abilities, to the core. Sir Thomas was still a member of the Institute of Civil Engineers, his floating trains continued to operate and locomotives passed over 300 miles of railway he had constructed in Scotland and England.

But now the bitter truth was that none of his achievements counted for anything. The Tay Bridge had fallen.

Sir Thomas retired to his country house in Moffat with Margaret Bouch and never left it for four months after the Report on the disaster which destroyed him. He died on November 1, 1880, from a cold which he had no will to resist and was buried in Edinburgh's Dean Cemetery ■

CONTENTS

BRIDGE ACROSS THE CENTURY:
The Story of the Forth Bridge

TEXT—**Sheila Mackay**
PRODUCTION—**Nic Allen**
DESIGN—**Harriet Wylie**
CONSULTANT EDITOR—**Richard Wilson**
ADVERTISING—**Margaret Wilson**

Printed in Scotland by Alna Press, Broxburn, West Lothian

Bridge Across The Century
ISBN 0 948473 00 2
First Published 1985. New Edition 1986

Photographs relating to the Forth Bridge's construction are reproduced by kind permission of British Railways (Scottish Region), the Scottish Record Office, the Royal Commission on the Ancient and Historical Monuments of Scotland and Edinburgh Public Libraries.

Cover photograph: Elton Collection, Ironbridge Gorge Museum Trust
Colour photography: Nic Allen

MOUBRAY HOUSE PRESS
53 High Street, Edinburgh EH1 1SR
Telephone: 031-556 4402

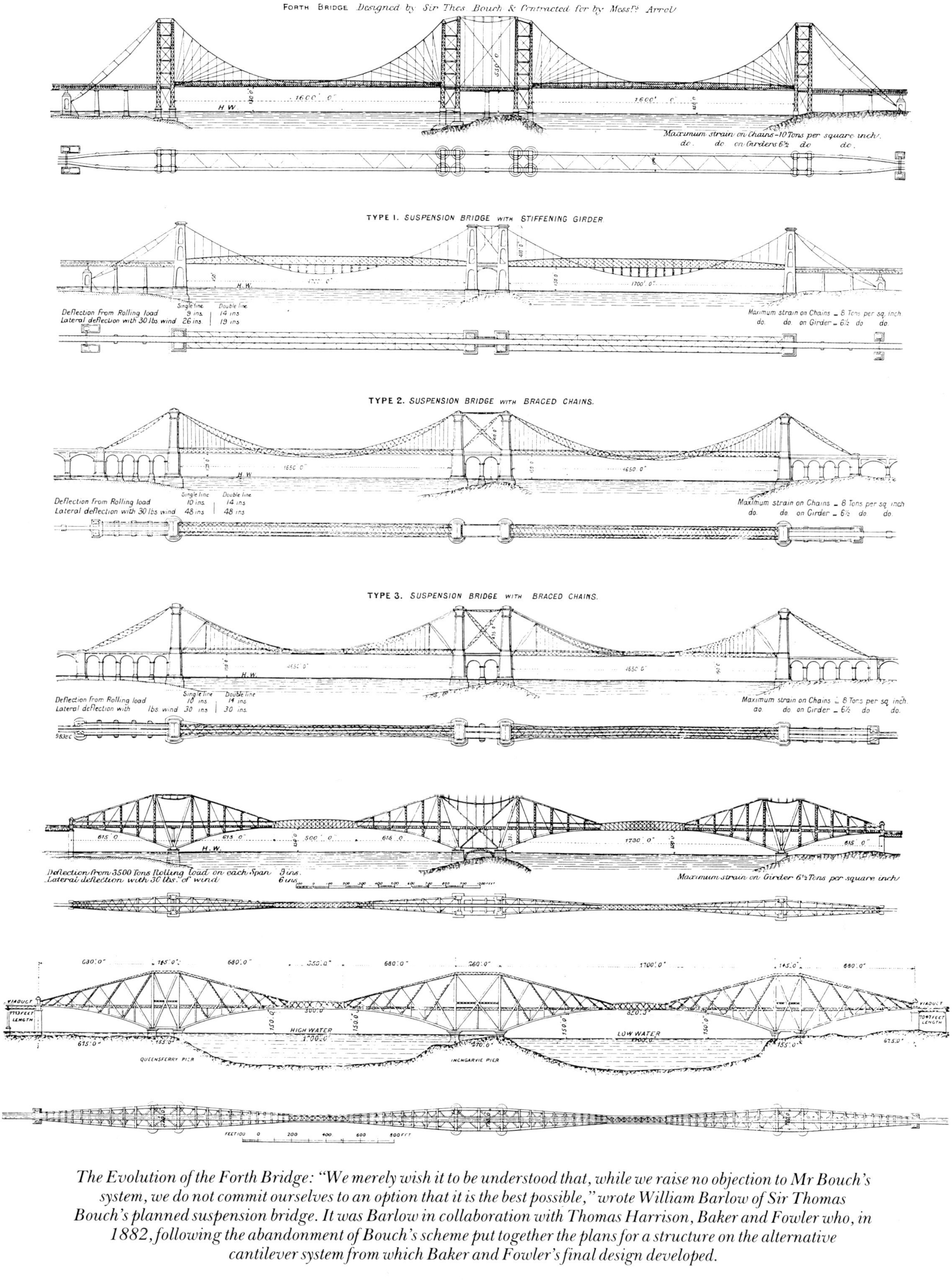

The Evolution of the Forth Bridge: "We merely wish it to be understood that, while we raise no objection to Mr Bouch's system, we do not commit ourselves to an option that it is the best possible," wrote William Barlow of Sir Thomas Bouch's planned suspension bridge. It was Barlow in collaboration with Thomas Harrison, Baker and Fowler who, in 1882, following the abandonment of Bouch's scheme put together the plans for a structure on the alternative cantilever system from which Baker and Fowler's final design developed.

THE CHASM BESIEGED

It would, however, have taken more than a disaster of this scale to halt a determined Victorian railway director in his tracks . . .

Before 1880 was out, the four railway companies had confirmed their intention to bridge the Forth and had instructed their consulting engineers, Messrs Barlow, Harrison and Fowler, to reconsider all the options. A design submitted by Fowler and Baker, based on the cantilever and central girder principle, was modified to take account of the conflicting views of other consultant engineers and submitted to the directors in May, 1881. From July, 1882, stocks and shares were taken up by the Midland, Great Northern, North Eastern and North British railway companies, and an Act of Parliament passed the same month authorised construction of the bridge with the stipulation that the Board of Trade should maintain an overall inspection of the works during construction.

Almost three years to the day after the Tay Bridge Disaster, on December 21, 1882, the contract for the construction of the Forth Bridge was awarded to Tancred, Arrol & Co. by the Forth Bridge Company. Aware that public anxiety in the wake of the Tay Bridge Disaster was still running high, the designers were determined that only the strongest materials would be used. Cast iron, used as a structural material on the Tay Bridge, was rejected in favour of steel: the Forth Bridge would be the first large structure built of steel. Intent on exploiting to the full the excellent properties inherent in this relatively new material, Fowler and Baker nevertheless retained caution. The structural steel would comply with specifications laid down by the Admiralty, Lloyd's, and the Underwriters' Registry—which were based on experience in using thousands of tons of steel plates, bars and angles in shipbuilding and similar work.

Soon after contracts were signed, a start was made on temporary work at both North and South Queensferry. Offices, stores, workshops and the No. 1 Shed, which had already been erected by William Arrol to back up work on Sir Thomas Bouch's abortive suspension bridge, were retained and bought over. Preparatory work for the construction of the foundations included fixing sites for the masonry piers which would eventually support the great cantilever towers. The foundations laid on the island of Inchgarvie by Thomas Bouch a decade earlier were ignored. Their crumbled remains still stand today, among Inchgarvie's other ruined memorials, the preserve of screeching sea-birds.

The Human Cantilever was devised by Baker to explain the cantilever principle at his Royal Institution lecture of 1887. It was described thus: "Two men sitting on chairs extend their arms, and support the same by grasping sticks which are butted against the chairs. There are thus two complete piers, as represented in the outline drawing above their heads. The centre girder is represented by a stick suspended or slung from the two inner hands of the men, while the anchorage provided by the counterpose in the cantilever end piers is represented here by a pile of bricks at each end. When a load is put on the central girder by a person sitting on it, the men's arms and the anchorage ropes come into tension, and the men's bodies from the shoulders downwards and the sticks come into compression. The chairs are representative of the circular granite piers. Imagine the chairs one-third of a mile apart and the men's heads as high as the cross of St Paul's, their arms represented by huge lattice steel girders and the sticks by tubes 12 feet in diameter at the base, and a very good notion of the structure is obtained".

The man supported by the two human cantilevers was Kaichi Watanabe, one of the first generation of Japanese engineers sent to study—and ultimately imitate and surpass—western technical achievements. Watanabe—a student of Fowler and Baker—was invited to participate in the human model of the cantilever to remind audiences of the debt the designers owed to the Far East where the cantilever principle was invented.

The Challenge: The site of the bridge viewed from the south in 1883. A jetty to facilitate work on the approach viaduct has been run out. Beyond lies the chasm to be bridged; the only encouragement offered by Nature being the 'stepping-stone' of Inchgarvie in the centre of the Firth.

THE SITE

The natural features offered by the chosen site were excellent: above both shores of the Firth, the land was sufficiently high to carry railway lines on to the approach-viaducts of the bridge while leaving adequate headroom for the largest naval and merchant ships; the water depth would allow the caissons, which formed a vital part of the foundations, to be sunk; the rocky promontory of the Fife or north shore offered a bedrock for one of the cantilevers as well as anchorage for barges and launches connected with the construction work; the whinstone island of Inchgarvie, overlaid with a bed of hard boulder clay, acted like a gigantic stepping stone on which to found the central or Inchgarvie cantilever.

A more promising site was impossible to imagine and, as if to allay any lingering anxiety, W. Westhofen, supervisor of works at the Inchgarvie cantilever, wrote these reassuring words early on in his splendid eye-witness account of the seven years' construction, which he called *The Forth Bridge:*

"There has been no single instance of the ground on which the foundations were placed being uncertain or in any way doubtful, and no anxiety need be felt in regard to this part of the Forth Bridge."

On a visit to the site in 1883, Benjamin Baker remarked on the bustle and activity both at Hawes Pier at Queensferry and on the north shore, which was such a contrast to the quietness, even dullness, which had characterised these places until then.

That year a cement store, general stores, cottages for the workmen, a large canteen and reading rooms were erected, and an observatory built at Port Edgar. The centre line of the bridge had been set out and the position of the masonry piers determined. Gas furnaces, engines, a large hydraulic accumulator, numerous cranes, drilling machines, a hydraulic crane and two large travelling cranes had been brought on site.

A wrought-iron landing-stage now stood on Inchgarvie and two others on the north shore where numerous cottages to house 90 foreign workmen, workshops and stores had been built. Air-compressing machinery, 576 holding-down bolts, 1,000 tons of steel plates and bars, 70,000 cubic feet of granite, were delivered to the sites where 38,000 cubic feet of concrete had been set and 5,000 yards laid.

By the end of the year the four main Fife piers were in hand. The south-west Queensferry pier was well advanced and ready for the caisson.

The construction of the bridge necessitated the building of a small town of workshops, offices and living quarters at South Queensferry. Drawings were made and models assembled in the vast Drawing Loft. Steel plates were curved to shape in a great 'Bending Press' and then assembled into the tubes which were to act as the principal members of the bridge on a series of Drill Roads beside the workshops.

THE MEN

As if in a gigantic military exercise, the engineers of the Railway Age marshalled troops of navvies into the construction of tracks, tunnels and bridges. The Forth Bridge operation was one of the largest of its type ever seen and, by the first year's end, workmen's cottages on both shores were filled to overflowing. Landing stages had been erected to bring in men and materials from all over Scotland, England, Ireland, Germany, France, Italy, Sweden and Japan.

The Scotsman recorded that Fowler had built a comfortable dwelling house where, besides a handsomely-furnished suite of apartments for his own occupation, there was accommodation for members of the resident staff. The engineers overlooked the bridge site and close to hand were an extensive model loft where patterns of actual working size could be handled, the immense workshop where the steel for the superstructure would be manipulated, and the yards and drill roads where the pieces of the world's longest bridge were assembled before being taken out to their final resting place.

Workmen arrived in droves, drawn by the promise of work aplenty.

Careful to recount the human as well as the technical side of the bridge-building story, Westhofen noted that a few of them were birds of passage who worked for a week or two and passed on, having contributed little to building progress but with full pay-packets in their pockets. Even during that first year, it was known all over the country that a free boat passage to Queensferry, North or South, could be easily obtained.

But the vast majority of the "briggers" were civilised and cooperative, coming in more or less equal numbers from Scotland, England and Ireland. Foreign workmen were employed in greater numbers when the caisson foundations were laid and again, in the final stages of construction, to lay the asphalt pavement along the railway line over the bridge which is still referred to as the permanent way.

In a year or two, accommodation for the briggers at Queensferry and

Above and Opposite page top: *The Workmen: At the height of construction 4,600 men were employed on the bridge. "Scotch, English and Irish were about equally represented as to numbers," wrote Westhofen, "and though the latter furnished very few skilled hands, they were mostly very hard workers and very conscientious and reliable men."*

North Queensferry had reached bursting point and the North British Railway Company laid on special workers' trains from Edinburgh, Inverkeithing and Dunfermline—two each morning and two each night. Later, the Edinburgh line was extended to Leith, where several hundred men chose to live rather than put up with overcrowded conditions nearer the site; this despite the fact that they had to leave Leith at 4 am, returning home at 7 pm.

On days when the weather was too bad for men to work on the bridge, the trains were turned back by telegraph, returning the men home rather than leaving them to hang about the Queensferry pubs.

They did a lot of sailing too. At first, a paddle-steamer was hired to take the briggers from shore to shore and to the foundation sites. Later it was replaced by a superior works vessel capable of carrying 450 men at a time and, gradually, a fleet of steam barges, launches and rowing boats was built up. Two rowing boats were attached to each cantilever as rescue boats which, during the seven years' construction, saved eight lives as well as 8,000 workmen's caps and other articles of clothing blown, or accidentally dropped, off the bridge.

Large shelters and dining rooms heated by stoves were provided on the ground and, later, even on top of the central towers at viaduct level and at the very ends of the cantilevers as the superstructure began to develop. This tradition persists on the bridge today, with four bothy groupings along the railway track. From the first summer, organisation of welfare for employees was impressive. A Sick and Accident Club was formed with compulsory membership at 8d (old pence) a week for every person engaged by Tancred & Arrol which itself contributed 22/- (old shillings) a year. Apart from the Club, the contractors supplied boots and waterproofs during work on the foundations, and later on, during the erection of the superstructure, thick woollen jackets, overalls and waterproof shoes.

The Directors of the Forth Bridge Railway Company on a site visit: The Directors were drawn equally from the four railway companies which came together to form the Forth Bridge Railway Company. They were the Marquis of Tweeddale and the Earl of Elgin (North British), Lord Colville and Lord Hindlip (Great Northern), John Dent and Sir Matthew Ridley (North Eastern), M. W. Thompson and W. Unwin Heygate (Midland). Behind them on one of the Drill Roads is the model of a skewback.

MEN OF STEEL

It is no wonder that those engineers of the old school can turn from one subject to another with so much versatility when we consider what an education they had. Instead of having professors to fill them with ready digested knowledge like the young men of the present day, they were moved from one position of responsibility to another, and their intellects were hardened and invigorated by constant work. Every step they took was an experiment on a working scale, and every fact they learned was imprinted on their memories by the toil and trouble it had cost.

W. Westhofen *in The Forth Bridge, 1890.*

BENJAMIN BAKER 1840-1907

The Designer

"If I were to pretend that the designing and building of the Forth Bridge was not a source of present and future anxiety to all concerned, no engineer of experience would believe me. Where no precedent exists, the successful engineer is he who makes the fewest mistakes."

In 1867 the young Benjamin Baker published a series of articles in *The Engineer* advocating the use of cantilevers supporting a girder system as the most effective means of providing long-span bridges. Considering the man he was, it is easy to imagine his real sense of humility at the twists of fate which 15 years later, after the abandonment of Bouch's Forth Bridge scheme, gave him the chance to convert his theory to reality on a gigantic stage.

It was a humility which derived from his knowledge of, and respect for, the pioneers of engineering—a respect which he demonstrated in his insistence that Telford's great Menai and Severn bridges be conserved and strengthened rather than replaced, and manifested itself in his suggestion that there were many other engineers capable of undertaking the construction of the Forth Bridge.

In fact, Baker was particularly well-qualified for the task before him. He combined a flair for engineering design with an understanding of the relevant materials gained in the most practical way—not through an academic schooling but by an apprenticeship served in the famous South Wales Ironworks at Neath Abbey which he entered at the age of 16.

On completing his training, he moved to London where he worked under W. H. Wilson on the construction of Victoria Station before joining the firm of John Fowler in 1862. He became a partner in 1875 and remained associated with the firm until Fowler's death in 1898, assuming responsibility for much of the work of the business.

Quite apart from the Forth Bridge, the work undertaken during these years was of epic proportions, even by the standards of Victorian engineering achievement. It is to Fowler and Baker, more than anyone else, that London owes its Underground railway network—which began as Fowler's Metropolitan Railway in the early 1860s and developed with Baker's pioneering work on the "tube" system in the 1890s.

Baker also acted as consulting engineer on the Aswan Dam (1894-1902) and assisted John Dixon in 1878 in the perilous business of transporting by sea, from Egypt to Britain, the great monolithic obelisk called Cleopatra's Needle.

He was remembered in old age by an employee: "In the office of Baker and Hutzig at Queen Square Place, I first saw, with his magnificent head, firm jaw, generous moustache and penetrating and fearless eyes; a most impressive figure, not by any means a big man; but a very great one . . ."

Baker was knighted for his work on the Forth Bridge in 1890.

WILLIAM ARROL 1839-1913

The Contractor

"Whatever I went to, I put my whole mind to . . ."

In the mid-1880s, when he was acting as contractor on the new Tay Bridge as well as the Forth Bridge, William Arrol would rise at five each Monday morning in his Glasgow home and be at his nearby Dalmarnock works at six to inspect progress.

He would then board the train for Edinburgh and the Forth Bridge, where he would work for the rest of Monday and Tuesday before catching the Dundee train to arrive at the Tay Bridge at about 11 pm. At six the following morning he would be at work there, returning late at night to Glasgow so that he could be back at his works first thing the following morning.

He would then travel again to the Forth and then the Tay before catching the train to London where, on Saturday, he would spend the day discussing progress with the consulting engineers. He would then return north unless business in London was incomplete in which case he would stay on through Sunday, making sure he visited Spurgeon's Tabernacle to hear the famous preacher.

Arrol was as ingenious as he was energetic. He had the ability constantly to think on the job. The riveting machines used on the Forth Bridge, for instance, were of his own design, developed specifically to overcome the particular problems of building this huge structure.

Energetic, ingenious, pious and rising to fame and a knighthood from humble origins, William Arrol was, indeed, the very stuff of Victorian dreams. He was born in Houston, Renfrewshire, the son of Thomas Arrol, a spinner. He went to work in a cotton mill at the age of nine and at 14 became a blacksmith's apprentice.

In 1863, he joined Laidlaw and Son, builder and bridge manufacturers in Glasgow and, in 1868, launched his own business on his life savings of just £85.

His hard work paid off. In 1872 he established the Dalmarnock Works and in 1875 undertook his first major construction, the building of the North British Railway bridge across the Clyde at Bothwell.

Arrol then went on to win the contract for Sir Thomas Bouch's abortive scheme for bridging the Forth and in 1882 became the successful tenderer for the greatest project of his career, Fowler and Baker's Forth Bridge.

This undertaking—and the building of the new Tay Bridge—were described by the Prince of Wales when he opened the Forth Bridge in 1890 as "monuments of his skill, resources and energy", and won him a knighthood in that year.

Meanwhile, in 1886, Arrol had begun work on London's Tower Bridge which was opened in 1894, once again by the Prince of Wales. And later contracts included the Nile Bridge at Cairo (1904-8) and the Wear Bridge at Sunderland (1905-9).

In 1885 he bought the estate of Seafield, near Ayr, where he built a house, tended the gardens and collected pictures until his death in February, 1913.

JOHN FOWLER 1817-1898

Born Sheffield. One of the great engineers in the age of Railwaymania, through which 'only men of iron constitution came unscathed'. Designer of Pimlico Bridge which carried the first railway across the Thames in 1860 and St Enoch's Station in Glasgow. Pioneer engineer of the London Underground system.

By the time that the Forth Bridge came to be built, Fowler had passed much of the responsibility for design to his younger colleague, Benjamin Baker. However, Fowler remained the senior partner throughout the period of construction and was rewarded with a baronetcy in 1890.

THE MATERIALS

That first year, machinery and plant of every description began to arrive on site and the pace was kept up at an astounding rate for the next five years at a cost not far short of half a million pounds. Much of it was specially designed or invented for the bridge works.

A siding to bring in delivery wagons was laid from Queensferry Station, and another alongside the workshops. Cranes were set up in every convenient position so that sections of raw steel, plates, bars, angles, tees and other hardware could be delivered quickly to the furnaces and drilling or planing machines.

The list of basic materials to build one of the wonders of the modern world read like this:

STEEL
: From the Welsh Landore Works, The Scottish Steel Company and Dalzell's Iron and Steel Works, Motherwell.

RIVETS
: Made by the Clyde Rivet Company.

GRANITE
: From Aberdeen.

RUBBLE
: From Arbroath.

WHINSTONE
: Quarried locally, or on site.

CONCRETE
: The whinstone on Inchgarvie and at North Queensferry was exclusively used and broken down by stone-breakers and crushers.

SAND
: Barges were sent 10 miles up the coast to Kinghorn and Pettycur, since local proprietors objected to the removal of sand from the foreshore.

CEMENT
: Exclusively Portland, manufactured on the Medway. An old hulk called the *Hougomont* brought it in and stored 10 or 12 tons at a time, moored off Queensferry. In 1886 the *Hougomont* was towed into Port Edgar after an outbreak of smallpox at Queensferry and converted into an isolation hospital.

TIMBER
: From Grangemouth in bulk—planks, battens and boards. Hardwoods including beech, oak and ash, from neighbouring sawmills.

CREOSOTE OIL
: Brought in by rail for the Lucigen lamps and rivet and other furnaces.

At the end of 1883, work was well underway on the construction of the masonry piers to support the north and south approach viaducts, including the building of coffer-dams and caissons. The caissons for Inchgarvie and North Queensferry were being constructed on the beach at Queensferry. Arrangements were complete for the electric lighting of the whole works.

From that first year, nothing was left to chance. Men and materials were directed with all the vigour and technical prowess that could be mustered from the engineers and supervisors. With so many false starts well behind them and the promise of the completion of this colossal pioneering structure ahead—no structure of anywhere near comparable size had ever been contemplated before—the men who built the bridge moved from foundations to superstructure at an astonishing pace ■

YEAR BY YEAR
THE WONDER GREW

From year to year the wonder grew, as the mighty piers slowly arose out of the sea and the ascending columns climbed ever higher and higher.
Sir Robert Purvis

The construction of the Forth Bridge fell into two equal parts — the years 1882-1886 were devoted to the sinking of the caissons and building of the piers on which the superstructure was to be founded. From 1886-1890 the superstructure itself was constructed, its progress visible for all to see from the shores of the Forth, as the Fife, Inchgarvie and Queensferry cantilevers rose higher and higher above the sea—finally to be joined by the massive girder arms.

The fears aroused by the Tay Bridge Disaster had led to considerable safety margins being incorporated in the Forth Bridge design and, although there was nothing new or untried in Fowler and Baker's cantilever design, it was revolutionary because of those linking girder arms . . . and its unprecedented colossal size.

The cantilever towers were designed to open out to a remarkable width of 120 feet at the masonry piers, so that the structure at railway-track level and above became light and compact in comparison. All manner of tests were carried out on models of the design which aimed at achieving maximum rigidity under the vertical stress of a moving train-load and under the horizontal stress of wind pressure, the Forth being particularly exposed to south-westerly gusts at the bridge site.

A fatal failure of the Tay Bridge had been its inability to withstand such excessive wind pressure, so the Forth Bridge engineers tested models on the outlandish assumption that a hurricane was blowing up one side of the Forth and down the other.

And Baker, practical as ever, insisted on taking part in experiments not only on wind pressure, but also on load pressure and tidal action. During the summer of 1882, wind pressure gauges were erected on top of the old castle on Inchgarvie and readings were taken right up to the bridge's completion in 1890.

Other vitally important factors the designers considered were ease and safety of erection, so that the unfinished structure was at all times during construction as invincible to the elements as the completed one would be. During erection, every stage of the work would provide the secure base from which the next stage could proceed, or a support from which temporary staging could be erected. It is a tribute to the supervisors that only 57 men died during the seven years of construction.

Before the contract was signed, the Board of Trade had insisted that the entire construction period be independently monitored to ensure the highest standards of workmanship and safety. Two engineers, a Major Marindan and a Major-General Hutchinson, were appointed to report quarterly from 1883 until February, 1890. Their reports appear in extracted form at the end of *Bridge Across the Century*. Together with the account written by Westhofen, they provide a wonderfully detailed report of month-by-month progress on the bridge.

Taking soundings off Inchgarvie, June 18, 1884.

FROM FOUNDATIONS TO SUPERSTRUCTURE

Only 18 months after the contract had been signed, the south-west Queensferry caisson was launched—on May 26, 1884, in the presence of Lord Aberdeen, Lord High Commissioner to the General Assembly of the Church of Scotland, and a large crowd which had gathered to watch the first of the several ceremonies which were to take place over the seven years' construction.

Things were moving so fast that, only one year later, Lord Aberdeen was back with his wife to take part in the ceremony to launch the sixth and *last* of the caissons founding the granite masonry piers upon which the superstructure still rests. After the party was received by the contractor's representatives, Sir Thomas Tancred and Joseph Phillips, Lady Aberdeen was invited to turn the lever of the hydraulic launching machine, allowing the north-west caisson to glide down the slips into the water where two tugs towed it out to the site . . . and a great cheer from the crowd accompanied this closing ceremony of the foundation works.

During 1885 two temporary bridges were built across the North British Railway line on the Queensferry side to connect with the Forth Bridge Works. The girders used fascinated the public, as they had been salvaged from a portion of the ill-fated Tay Bridge. Offices were extended and drill roads added to. A new drawing loft was erected and the steel work plant augmented. And as progress on the main masonry piers went forward at a pace, impromptu inventions were made to deal with the problems as they arose.

On one occasion, Mr Arrol visited an air chamber in a caisson to see what could be done to hurry up the work—and quickly invented a hydraulic spade. But the main feature of the year was the unfortunate accident in which two men were killed when the fitted Queensferry caisson burst while being pumped out.

At the beginning of 1886 a large amount of material for the superstructure had already been prepared: "The whole of the bridge is built in large sections in the works at Queensferry and the rivet fixtures tried so that no difficulty may be experienced in fitting up when the material is sent out to the piers," reported *The Scotsman*; adding with some suprise: "It thus comes about that the whole of the bridge will have been twice built er it is finally erected."

All the temporary work during the year consisted of making appliances to assist the erection of the

CAISSONS:
Vital, but what *ARE* they?

For all its ingenuity of design, the magnificent superstructure of the Forth Bridge is only as stable as the groups of four platforms on which the cantilever towers stand; and where these platforms rest on underwater foundations, the key to success is in each case a 400-ton, 70-feet-diameter, wrought-iron cylinder known as a CAISSON.

The principle of the caisson is straightforward, but its operation in this case involved highly hazardous work on an epic scale. The caissons were assembled on South Queensferry beach then floated out to the position of each of the cantilever tower platforms. Concrete was then poured into them until they sank to the estuary bed. A temporary dam was built around the top of each cylinder to facilitate work above the caisson while, at the bottom, a steel cutting edge around the circumference extended some seven feet below the concrete-filled floor.

There was now only one way to secure the foundations of the caisson . . .

The water in the chamber between the concrete and the river-bed was pumped out and, in order to ensure that the pressure at that depth did not allow it to re-enter, it was replaced by compressed air. Shafts—each with an air-lock to maintain the compressed atmosphere below—led to what now became a working chamber. Down iron rungs in

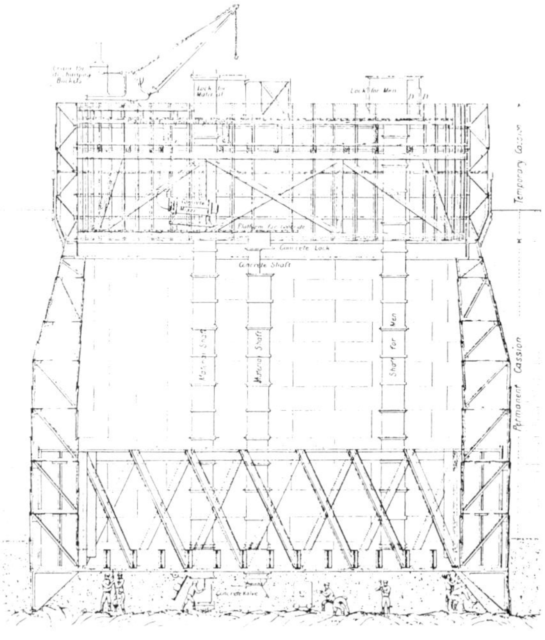

one of these shafts descended workmen whose job it was to secure a firm base for each caisson by, quite literally, digging away at the very foundations on which they stood.

Once their efforts had sunk the caissons to the required depth, the working chambers were filled with concrete, masonry-piers built above, the temporary dam around these piers removed, and the foundations made ready to receive the steel bedplates to which the superstructure would be secured ■

cantilevers: hydraulic apparatus for riveting and lifting, specially-designed machines for riveting the steel tubular members, Goliath cranes, hoists and steam-winders, compressors, accumulators, rams for high-pressure riveting, were all made ready. Three thousand men were employed now, and by the end of the year 33,000 tons of steel had been delivered to the site.

The 12 solid foundation piers in three groups of four were now finished at the top with courses of granite masonry. The lowest part of each cantilever tower was constructed: steel plates held down by foundation bolts going down to a depth of 26 feet within the foundation piers; four layers of steel plates on each cantilever base, each weighing about 100 tons. The skewback was then fixed on each pier to hold together the 10 component members of the cantilever.

As Mr Biggart—who was in charge of the drawing offices, shops and yards—reported in a paper he read to the Institute of Engineers and Shipbuilders in Scotland a year before the bridge was finished, the skewbacks were the most complicated parts of the entire bridge superstructure:

"Each skewback is a starting point or a termination of five separate tubes and five distinct box girders . . . the difficulties (are) mostly on account of the various angles at which the different parts lie in relation to one another and the skewback."

The engineers invented special appliances for riveting these skewbacks which acted as the upper or sliding bed-plates which would bear some of the movement of the piers and cantilevers, due to expansion and contraction. The erection of the vertical cantilever columns was performed by means of a platform supported by the columns themselves and carried up with them, one on each side of the axis of the bridge.

In the workshops on each shore, drilling and fitting of materials for the internal viaduct—where the railway line, or permanent way would be laid—was well in hand. By July, the Fife cantilever was well advanced and the north approach-viaduct piers had been carried up to within a few feet of their ultimate height.

A start was made with building out the bottom tubular steel members of each of the cantilever arms at the same time as the cantilever towers were being constructed upwards. But the members of the top cantilever arms could not be started until the full height of each cantilever had been reached in 1887.

Previous page: *Launching the last caisson for Inchgarvie south-west cantilever, May 29, 1885.*
Above: *Working on top of one of the Inchgarvie caissons, April 1884.*

1887—MOMENTOUS YEAR

The year that Queen Victoria celebrated 50 years of rule, the three cantilever columns reached their final, majestic height. Now the task was to *join* the Queensferry, Inchgarvie and Fife cantilevers, and so work began on building out the bottom tubular steel members north and south from the columns. Progress was visible and measurable—in terms of the distance these bottom members (and later, the top members) had reached from the cantilever columns.

Crowds watched breathlessly from the shore as the central girder arms were constructed by men and machines suspended between sea and sky. As Sir Robert Purvis exclaimed in his *Memoir* of Sir William Arrol:

More and more was the amazement as, week by week, the columns were perceived to be throwing out enormous, far-reaching growths on either side. Each of these was ever increasing in weight and altering in shape but ever in perfect balance.

The bridge site had become a shrine to industry which any engineer worth his salt in Europe, Asia, Africa or America aspired at least to visit. Ever since the visit of the Prince and Princess of Wales in August, 1884, hardly a week had passed without a visit from, as Westhofen put it, "one-tenth of all people distinguished by rank or by scientific or social attainments".

The distinguished roll-call included the Emperor of Brazil, the Kings of Saxony and Belgium, the King of Sweden, the Marquis Tseng of China, and the Shah of Shahs.

Not content to view the wonder of the age from the shore, these "hundreds of visitors, men of science of all nations, turbanned Indian princes and even venturesome young ladies", climbed all over the structure.

"As in most other matters," wrote Westhofen, "ladies were to the fore, pluckily climbing into every nook and corner where anything interesting might be seen or learned, up the hoists and down the stairs and ladders, and frequently leaving the members of the so-called stronger sex far behind. It is needless to say that, under such circumstances, the duties of those called upon to guard the fair visitors were of the most agreeable."

Visitors were actively encouraged on site in a way which is impossible to imagine in our ultra-safety-conscious society, and Benjamin Baker took great pleasure in the sport afforded by an ascent to the top of the towers he had designed. For him, it was all a great human experience—in Jubilee Year he first demonstrated the cantilever principle using human models, which captured the imagination of people all over the world and which was endlessly reproduced in newspapers and periodicals of the day. He also travelled and lectured extensively, both at home and abroad, throughout the years of the bridge's construction. An imaginative and tireless educator, he relished capturing just the right analogy through which to communicate. In his 1887 lecture to the Edinburgh Literary Institute Baker suggested to his audience a way of grasping the enormous size of the Forth Bridge:

"To get an idea of the spans, let them stand on Waverley Bridge and look towards the Castle, and consider that the engineers had to span that distance with a complicated structure weighing 150,000 tons without the possibility of any intermediate pier or support; and let them consider also that their rail level would be as high above the sea as the Castle esplanade was above Princes Street, and that the steelwork of the bridge would soar 200 feet higher . . ."

For a London audience the same year, he translated the Edinburgh place-names to Green Park, Piccadilly and St. Paul's Cathedral.

A reporter from the *Dundee Advertiser* was one of the visitors who climbed the cantilevers that year. There were two ways to go: you could reach the upper platforms by a staircase or by a cage rapidly drawn through the air by steam power. He chose the latter and wrote:

"The cage is a small steel framework in which half-a-dozen persons may stand, but as it travels up through space, it resembles a canary cage. Once in it, visitors are as helpless as eggs in a basket and the sensation of being rapidly drawn through the air, up, up and

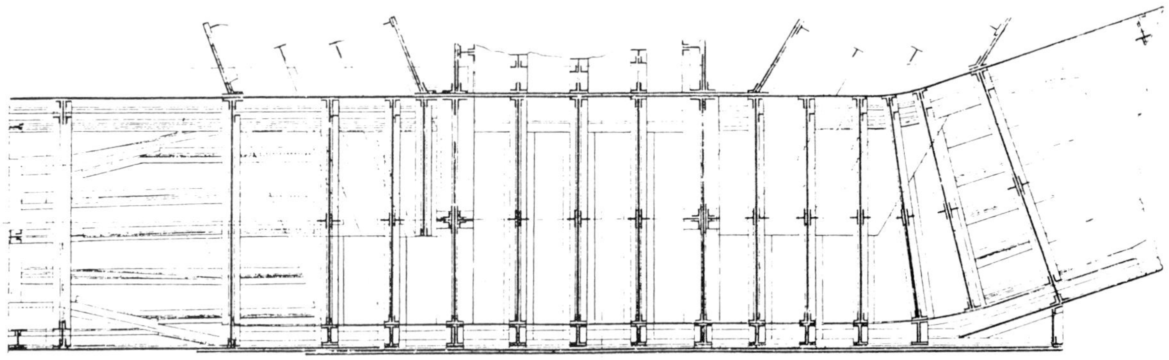

The Skewbacks: Once the caissons had been completed, massive steel bedplates, 37 feet long by 17 feet wide, were fixed to the top surface of all twelve of them. A skewback was attached to each bedplate—the assemblage of steel tubes from which sprung all the supporting members of the bridge. The skewbacks were therefore of great importance. They were the element which ultimately transferred the weight of the bridge's superstructure on to the supporting foundations. Westhofen's diagram shows the way in which they were assembled while a full-size model of the skewback is to be seen in the background of the photograph of the Bridge Directors (p. 9).

still up, is peculiar . . . when the top is gained, and when a ladder is climbed ascending to the upper platforms, a magnificent view is obtained. A grand idea is also had of the stupendous nature of the Bridge works . . . From this upper platform one can gaze into the mouths of the great steel tubes. Their twelve feet of diameter look more, so massive and strong do they seem."

Benjamin Baker thought the view from "the summit" was sublime. And Westhofen, looking out from the top of the Inchgarvie cantilever which was his particular responsibility, described the river beneath and the surrounding countryside in ecstatic terms. On a fine day the river beneath was alive with a flotilla of pleasure boats and paddle steamers, merchant and Navy vessels, fishing boats, and the barges and launches connected with the construction of the bridge.

He could see May Island 35 miles away towards the north of the estuary at the North Sea. The Bass Rock and Berwick Law, the East Lothian Coast and the ridge of the Lammermuir Hills; Inchkeith, Inchcolm, Inchmikery and Cramond Island; Leith Harbour, Granton, Newhaven, Edinburgh, Arthur's Seat, the Pentland Hills, Linlithgow, Bo'ness, Grangemouth, the Campsie Fells, the Ochil Hills, wooded shores, farms, towns and villages, and Ben Lomond 60 miles to the west—all were encompassed in his spectacular view from the Inchgarvie cantilever.

During night shift on the bridge, the vast surrounding darkness was punctuated by the flashing lights of the island lighthouses, the harbour lights of Granton, Leith, Newhaven and Burntisland. Sometimes up to 200 vessels were anchored in the Firth, the long struggling lines of their masthead lights giving the appearance of a busy town having suddenly risen from the waters.

At the height of the construction in Victoria's Jubilee Year, more than 4,000 men were employed round the clock. Jubilee night itself, on June 21, the longest day of the year, was hazy. Even so, 68 bonfires were counted on the surrounding hills and landmarks. As usual, the great central towers of the cantilevers were lit by hundreds of electric arc-lights at various heights where work was carried on, and each cantilever was reflected again in the water. They resembled three pillars of fire rising from the sea—an unforgettable spectacle to the crowds gathered on both shores of the Forth to celebrate the Queen's 50-year reign.

The celebrations marked a turning point. With the construction of the three cantilevers, the dream of the pioneering engineers was close to becoming reality.

All that remained was to close the gaps.

Looking north from the top of the Inchgarvie cantilever, August 18, 1887: "When the top is gained and when a ladder is climbed ascending to the upper platforms, a magnificent view is obtained. A grand idea is also had of the stupendous nature of the Bridge works."

Dundee Advertiser, *1887*

BRIDGING THE GAPS

The nation was now avid for any news of the bridge's progress towards completion and the newspapers and periodicals of the day obliged readers with regular and extensive reports. Readers of *The Scotsman* learned about the process in which the bridge acted as a scaffolding for its own construction, since freestanding scaffolding could not be erected over the water for work on the cantilevers:

The workers today are practically standing upon their labours of yesterday. As soon as a fresh round of steel plates is added to the tubes, or an additional girder section rivetted to the top arms, the platforms with their freight of men and cranes and other mechanical appliances are slid out correspondingly and a new piece of work is begun which again, when completed, will give the necessary standing support for a further extension . . . Every piece of work done becomes the basis of another advance, and the Forth Bridge men labour much in the same way as the Esquimaux who ascends the ice-cliff by cutting steps, one after another in its face.

March 1888

In May, 1888, a reporter from *The Builder* described how the steel cantilever members had to be built out on either side of the cantilever towers at the same rate to hold the whole in equilibrium:

The whole work, as we saw it from the engineers' steam launch, has a most remarkable appearance at present. The three piers (cantilever towers) suggesting the idea of three enormous ships with the tubes projecting like gigantic bowsprits over the water, and everything at present hanging out into the air unsupported.

"And so night and day the work goes on, for when the sun goes down hundreds of electric lamps light up the great cantilevers," reported the *Bradford Observer*, adding that "in all but very stormy weather, the work may be said to be continuous, save on Sundays."
Taking the story further, *The Scotsman* reported:

At the ends of the cantilevers are large platforms above and below on which the men work . . . the upper platform carries two cranes . . . one for raising and lowering the pieces of steel into their places, and another that bears an immensely powerful hydraulic rivetting machine. This machine, which is not unlike a pair of shears, has been specially designed by Mr Arrol for the work. It exerts a pressure of forty tons and squeezes and welds the steel bolts as if they were made of clay.

Throughout the construction of the cantilevers, the gigantic steel tubes which formed them were fitted together in Queensferry, taken out by works vessels and placed in situ by cranes, hoists and riveting machines. The men worked at this stage from cages which encircled and slid along the tubes to replace bolts with rivets. Finally, the gigantic projecting steel tubes were joined by extending a continuous girder between them.
There was a gap of 350 feet between each cantilever after their arms, north and south, had been built to full length. The suspended girders which would now be attached were thus about 350 feet long and 40 feet high at the ends and 50 feet high in the centre—though highly exact measurements were made, taking into account anticipated expansion in the heat of the sun. Each girder was divided into eight slightly unequal lengths. Their erection on the superstructure to close the gaps between the cantilevers was a precise and highly-organised operation. All the arms were finished by July, 1889. The month before, the south arm of the Queensferry cantilever had been so close to the approach-viaduct that planks could be laid across to allow the directors of the Forth Bridge Railway Company to walk from the south shore to the northern arm of the Queensferry cantilever.
Efforts to complete the bridge reached fever pitch as the briggers on the Fife and Queensferry cantilevers vied with each other to become the first to cross to the Inchgarvie cantilever.
Strong temporary platforms projecting some 25 feet beyond the end of the cantilevers were attached to the underside of the bottom members where the first half-bay of the suspended girder was erected. The girders were built out from the closing structure, half a bay at a time, each joint in the top and bottom boom being riveted before extra weight was added forward.
When the fifth bay had been added, the cantilevers were so narrow that the twin cranes which had done much of the lifting work could not be taken out further. The heavy platforms they carried were removed to make them lighter as they climbed up the curve of the girder arm towards the middle of the span. From here, the cranes lifted material from barges in mid-stream; and the heavy floor girders (four tons each) were hoisted up by special tackle with wire ropes and steam-winches set up near the ends of the cantilever arms.
In September a wily brigger placed a ladder between the jibs of the cranes working on the cantilever arms and made a dangerous crossing 200 feet above water, from Queensferry to Inchgarvie cantilever.
By October 10 the gap was structurally closed.
And on October 15 the workmen cheered directors and their friends on their walk across to Fife—only a 60 feet gap remained between the Inchgarvie and Fife cantilevers which had been temporarily bridged by a wooden structure for the occasion. Miss Constance

Top left: *View looking through the finely symmetrical stonework of the Jubilee Arch where the Forth Bridge was declared open by the Prince of Wales in 1890.* ***Top right:*** *View from the top of Inchgarvie cantilever looking towards Fife.* ***Middle left:*** *Jim Sinclair, the bridge supervisor, pauses during a routine inspection on the ladder which links the cantilever piers with the railway line on the bridge above. Inchgarvie island lies below.* ***Middle right:*** *The painting job is never-ending. Here, a section has been freshly coated with red oxide of iron paint.* ***Bottom left:*** *The Hawes Inn was at the centre of bridge-building activity. Its bars gave sustenance to briggers and its "pretty gardens of Hawthorns" provided an accident ward in emergencies.* ***Bottom right:*** *A south approach viaduct masonry pier.*
Centre spread: *Looking north from the Inchgarvie West Caisson. The lighthouse, erected in 1887, stands on a brick pier, the only remnant of Thomas Bouch's doomed scheme for a gigantic suspension bridge.*

Taylor, a niece of the Marquess of Tweeddale, Chairman of the North British Railway Company, was the first person across, escorted by the chairman of the Forth Bridge Railway Company.

A few months later, her uncle was to drive the first train across the completed bridge.

By October 28 the last booms were in and, by November 6, the north-central girder was ready to be connected, a process which required a rise in temperature and consequent expansion of the girder to allow the key-plates to fall into place. Westhofen was on hand to record the emotional moment of the bridge's completion:

The temperature on that day did not rise sufficiently high to make the joint, but in the night a sudden rise took place, and by 7.30 in the morning the bottom booms were joined together for good.

It now required a good fall of the temperature to get the top booms connected [because they were on a camber] . . . But the weather remained obstinate and it was not until the morning of November 14 that the key-plates could be driven in and the final connection made . . .

And thus the Forth Bridge was completed—for the remaining work was simply to replace temporary connections by permanent ones, to rivet up those which were only bolted, and do the thousand and one things which always remain to be done after everything is said to be finished.

The thrilling portion of the story is done, and the novelist would wish to leave off with so dramatic an incident as that just told. But there are yet some details which belong to the history of the bridge, and which could not very well be left unrecorded . . .

Indeed, the completed Forth Railway Bridge was subjected to severe tests before it was finally declared open in March, 1890.

On January 21, two trains were taken on to the bridge. Their gross weight of 1,800 tons was made up of 100 coal wagons and six locomotives of 73 tons apiece. The trains were moved slowly abreast and halted three-quarters of the way through the central girder connecting Queensferry with Inchgarvie cantilever. Sir John Fowler and Benjamin Baker also took readings at other points along the bridge and were quite satisfied that the structure was adequately stiff in all directions.

This happy conclusion, combined with the bridge's easy withstanding of heavy gales before and after the loading tests, prompted the Board of Trade inspectors to report that "this great undertaking, every part of which we have seen at different stages of its construction, is a wonderful example of thoroughly good workmanship with excellent materials, and both in its conception and execution is a credit to all who have been connected with it" ■

View looking through viaduct girders with briggers working from a temporary platform.

UPWARDS AND

AUGUST 1884

MAY 1886

APRIL 1887

OCTOBER 1887

JUNE 1888

OCTOBER 1888

OUTWARDS

JUNE 1886

MARCH 1887

EARLY 1888

JUNE 1888

JUNE 1889

THE BRIDGE COMPLETE

THE COST IN MEN'S LIVES

The building of the Forth Bridge cost a total of 57 lives. Grim though this toll might seem to be, it provided a fair cause for relief on the part of the engineers and contractors who realised just how much worse it could have been on a structure which involved extensive work both below sea-level and at great heights.

The lack of accidents during the caisson operations was a particular relief, given the danger of the work. The men in the caissons quite literally dug away at the foundations on which they stood; if the caisson sunk too quickly, they could all too easily be squashed between the sea-bed below and the thousands of tons of concrete immediately above them.

Baker had every reason to be apprehensive, for he was aware of the terrible fate of the workers in the caissons below the waters of the Neva at St Petersburg a few years before—in 1876—when one caisson suddenly sank 18 inches. Of the 28 men in the chamber, nine remained imprisoned and only two were taken out alive. The rest were smothered in the mud.

Baker was also aware of the dangers of men working in compressed air below sea-level, from his knowledge of accidents in the previous decade during the construction of New York's Brooklyn Bridge and the St Louis Bridge—119 of the 600 employed in the caisson there were affected by the 'bends'. Sixteen died and two were permanently crippled.

It was therefore a remarkable achievement that, during the building of the Forth Bridge, not a single man died while working under the caissons on the sea-bed—though there were some close shaves. On one occasion a few men were buried up to their chins in the mud, and on another, a caisson suddenly dropped seven feet while men were working underneath.

The only deaths associated with the construction of the foundations occurred when the Queensferry north-west caisson ruptured while being pumped out. The sea rushed in and two men were killed. The story is sometimes heard of another two men trapped beyond rescue under a caisson, who were fed poisoned food to put them out of their misery—but it seems to be apocryphal.

It is impossible to carry out a gigantic work without paying for it not merely in money, but in men's lives.

Benjamin Baker

Working at a height was a different matter, however. It became impossible to avoid accidents. As the superstructure rose higher and higher, so did the number of deaths. The grim toll was coldly recorded in the Board of Trade Reports:

AUGUST, 1887: *"Seven deaths."*

NOVEMBER, 1887: *"Eight fatal accidents among the workmen during the past quarter, two having been killed during a gale of wind by a plank blown some distance from the North Queensferry pier. We were informed that none of the accidents was due to any failure of plant, such as has caused accidents in previous quarters."*

AUGUST, 1888: *"Four fatal accidents during the quarter; one of these occurred to the engineer of one of the screw steamers, and is not attributable to the nature of the work; in another case, a rigger's help missed his footing and fell against a hand-rail which gave way. This was therefore a preventable accident as the hand-rail should have been more substantial."*

NOVEMBER, 1888: *"Six deaths, but none appear to have been due to any want of care on the part of the contractors."*

AUGUST, 1889: *"One fatal accident which we are informed was due to the workman's own want of caution."*

NOVEMBER, 1889: *"We regret to report that even with (the) reduced number of workers, there have been four fatal accidents, one of which, on September 12th when a rivetter, John Aitken, aged 16, was killed, was due apparently to carelessness in the fixing of a stage upon which he was working. Two others, on the 18th and 24th September, are stated to have been due to the falling of pieces of wood from a height, which should not occur if proper care be taken. In the fourth case a rigger unfortunately lost his balance and fell into the water, receiving fatal injuries."*

The fearsome momentum gained by objects falling from heights on the bridge filled the engineers with awe. Baker reported having seen a hole straight through a four-inch-thick timber caused by a spanner dropped 300 feet. On another occasion, a spanner entered a brigger's waistcoat and exited through his trouser leg, ripping his clothes apart but leaving him uninjured.

Baker also noted that a man who failed to close the rail on a hoist, stumbled and fell backwards a distance of 180 feet, "carrying away a dozen rungs of a ladder with which he came in contact, as if they had been straws".

An accident in June, 1887, brought about the only serious strike during the building of the bridge. When attempts were made to move a stage which had become jammed in a girder, it collapsed, killing two men and a boy and injuring three others. The briggers downed tools for a week, demanding an extra penny an hour—which would have constituted a 15 to 20 per cent rise—as danger money.

The supervisors countered that most of the accidents which took place were the result of carelessness—the consequence, said Baker, of a familiarity with danger which bred a certain contempt for it. Drink was another problem. There were many dead and injured who, in Baker's estimation, would have escaped "had it not been for the whisky of the Hawes Inn" ■

"The Hawes Inn flourishes too well for being in the middle of our works, its attractions prove irresistible for a large proportion of our 3,000 workmen. The accident ward adjoins the pretty garden with hawthorns, and many dead and injured men have been carried there, who would have escaped had it not been for the whisky of the Hawes Inn."

Benjamin Baker, 1887.

THE PAINTING JOB THAT NEVER ENDS

Everyone is fascinated by how the Forth Bridge is painted. When it was under construction, four firms were asked to tender as suppliers and samples of paint to the same specifications were tried out on the three cantilevers and the central girders. One of these firms, Craig & Rose of Leith, won the maintenance contract and has supplied its Forth Bridge Oxide of Iron Brushing Paint ever since.

As soon as they passed through the workshops or yards, every part of the superstructure—plates, bars, angles and tubes—received a good scraping down and a coat of boiled linseed oil. Then, when erected on the structure, they were coated with red lead paint. The insides of the tubular members received one coat of red and two coats of white lead paint. No less than 35,527 gallons of paint oils and 250 tons of paint were used during the building of the bridge.

The early bridge painters, men fresh from the clipper ships, would shin up the exposed surfaces of the cantilevers, rope in one hand, paintbrush in the other. Today, the 16 bridge painters are hauled up and down on hydraulic lifts or cradles which meet Government safety requirements. In the "climbing season", between April and September, they literally hang round the tubular members above the railway line and cling on with their legs, since it is impossible to erect scaffolding above the railway line.

It takes three days and three nights to make a batch of Forth Bridge paint. But 100 gallons are always kept in store in case of demand for the painters make the most of any sudden spells of dry and settled weather. Spirits, gel, synthetic resins, natural red oxide, barytes and talc are the magic ingredients which are blended in a huge ball mill, tile-lined and filled with pebbles and granite stones, kept specially for the purpose in Craig & Rose's Leith mills.

The painting area is estimated to be 145 acres, and 7,000 gallons would be needed to paint the bridge from end to end. Contrary to what practically everyone believes, it never is; though it does get done over regularly in a rough cycle of four to six years. And it is bound to be looking its immaculate best for the centenary celebrations in 1990.

THE FORTH BRIDGE IS OPENED

'All Reap at Last the Actions they have Sown . . .'

Nothing was spared by way of Victorian homily, ingenuity, or expense, to celebrate at last the opening of the Forth Bridge on Tuesday, March 4, 1890. The lavishly-decorated souvenir menu declared: *Of dazzling great adventures, this, the foremost.* And the steam train above the caption was aptly called *Progress*, for the whole exercise represented, as *Industries* magazine observed in a Forth Bridge Special, a dramatic shrinking of the earth's surface, bringing its inhabitants yet closer together.
The royal party arrived at 11.30 am by special train, to be received at the Forth Bridge Station—now Dalmeny—by Fowler, Baker, Arrol, and all the directors of the Forth Bridge Railway Company.
Then, undaunted by the cold, blustery weather, they fulfilled a demanding two-hour-long schedule which comprised a boat trip from North Queensferry under the bridge and round Inchgarvie island, and a return trip across the bridge with two stops—one to allow the Prince of Wales to drive home the last of seven million rivets; and another at the Queensferry cantilever where, from a specially-erected platform, he said simply: "Ladies and gentlemen, I now declare the Forth Bridge open."
For the splendid lunch and honours which followed, the engineers' model loft was transformed into a banqueting hall; strips of white calico, edged with blue and red, concealed the wooden roof, and a magnificent canopy of crimson and gold velvet was decorated with the Royal Coat of Arms and the motto of the Prince of Wales on a gold scroll.
Shields bearing the arms of British towns, and those of the great railway companies, added further embellishment to a building which, for the previous seven years, had been solely devoted to utilitarian—albeit grandly ambitious—purposes.
There could have been no more fitting time and place for the announcement that William Thompson, chairman of the Forth Bridge and Midland Railway Companies, and Fowler, were to be made baronets, and that Baker and Arrol were to be knighted—the first of a host of honours which were to come their way, both at home and abroad, in the years that followed ■

UBIQUITOUS BRIDGE

The visit of the Shah of Shahs.

From the moment its superstructure began to rise out of the sea, the bridge attracted thousands of sightseers, and in 1890—despite competition from the Edinburgh Exhibition on a 50-acre site featuring attractions such as an electrical display, a music hall and a Japanese village—the Forth Bridge was the runaway tourist attraction.
People were reluctant to travel over it at first, but there was no doubting their admiration for it. Though some Victorians lamented the lack of artistic embellishment on the structure, Royal Academician Alfred Waterhouse wrote to John Fowler: "One feature especially delights me—the absence of all ornament. Any architectural detail borrowed from any style would have been out of place in such a work. As it is, the bridge is a style unto itself: the simple directness of purpose with which it does its work is splendid and invests your vast monument with a kind of beauty of its own, differing though it certainly does from all the beautiful things I have ever seen."
Inevitably, the bridge had its detractors. Historian and art critic John Ruskin was vociferous in his loathing of it and William Morris called it "the supremist specimen of all ugliness".
Ever on the alert to counter such critics, however, Benjamin Baker wrote in *The Builder* in 1888: "The Eiffel Tower is a foolish piece of work, ugly, ill-proportioned and of no real use to anyone. The Forth Bridge is a work of usefulness (which has been) stigmatised as very ugly, but it has the beauty and expressiveness of naked construction of a scientific stamp."
Yet criticism continued long after Baker's death. Twenty years after the opening of the bridge, the author of a book about it deplored the fact that the cantilevers had been "cut off bluntly at the top" in the interests of utilitarian function, adding that the addition of gilt paint might have rendered it more glamorous.
In our own time, however, Sir Kenneth Clark firmly set the Forth Bridge in the tradition of the great artistic and philosophical achievements of the civilisation of mankind, and chose the bridge to illustrate the cover of his magnum opus—*Civilisation*.
The Forth Bridge has never ceased to inspire wonder and affection in the popular imagination. Throughout the 20th century it has been used countless times—the ubiquitous symbol *par excellence* of strength, reliability and permanence—to advertise everything from shortbread and ladies' stockings, to banking systems and microelectronics ■

Previous page: *Front cover of the lavishly designed menu, toasts and honours list, given to guests at Opening Ceremony.* ***Above:*** *Back cover of menu.*

WALKING THROUGH THE BRIDGE TODAY

One of the greatest railway journeys in the world is also the shortest. It takes just over 10 minutes to reach the Forth Bridge from Edinburgh's Waverley Station, and a good few less than that to pass under the Jubilee Arch and traverse the interior of this pinnacle of Victorian engineering achievement . . .

British Rail regretfully turns down many requests from *aficionados* each year, many of them Americans, who are eager to walk the bridge from end to end and appreciate the complexity of its construction more intimately than they can from a train. But in the interests of uninterrupted maintenance and safety, visits are restricted to engineers and groups with a professional interest, such as railway preservation societies and Permanent Way institutions.

On average, one visit a week is conducted over the bridge, frequently by Jim Sinclair, the bridge supervisor. For the lucky few, it goes something like this . . .

Indemnity forms signed, regulation orange fluorescent half-jackets donned and safety instructions received, they set out on the walk of one mile, 1,005 yards over the bridge from North Queensferry to Dalmeny Station.

As if on cue, the first train approaches the Fife cantilever and gives a blast of the horn. Jim lifts an arm in recognition and signals the party to stand in against the railing as one of the 200 trains which use the bridge every 24 hours lumbers past: speeds vary between 30 and 50 mph, depending on the type of the train.

Still over terra firma, above the north-approach masonry piers, it is nevertheless a long way down to the village of North Queensferry from the narrow bridge walkway which runs alongside the railway track, or permanent way.

The village once bustled with bridge-making activity and a living link with that period is Robert Douglas (96), who several years ago published *Ferry Yarns*, a delightful account of his childhood lived out under the great growing arches:

View of the bridge's underbelly: seldom seem but every bit as exciting in construction as the high girders.

"My father was the first carpenter on the Forth Bridge . . . we children felt as if the quality of our lives was enhanced by the association".
There's a bird's-eye-view of the whinstone outcrop below the village, and of the high-speed launch moored there which British Rail maintains for emergencies: George Cuthbertson and Bob Dowie are based in a porta-cabin nearby, on stand-by rescue duty in case a painter or maintenance worker falls from the bridge. To stay on their toes, they test out the inflatable craft twice a day, zooming out to the central cantilever and back in next to no time.
They have never yet been in a life-or-death dash—which is just as well, since the bridge-walker, looking below with trepidation, hardly needs telling that no-one has fallen from here and survived.
"I never cease to marvel at the technical brilliance that went into creating this bridge," says Jim Sinclair as the party proceeds south. After 12 years as bridge foreman, Jim was appointed bridge supervisor in 1979 and works from an office at Dalmeny Station. "It's amazing that, almost a century later, she's as good as new. No major structural repairs have been necessary. We've replaced some bracings and angle-plates which got corroded by smoke and steam blasts from the old locomotives, that's all."
There is a world of difference between walking over the bridge and rumbling through it on a train. Up here, suspended between sea and sky by a maze of red girders and spans, there's a tangible peace—between trains. The workmen would become complacent if they knew the train timetables by heart, so they learn instead to be ever-vigilant.
Forty men work up here in a world apart: sixteen painters, two carpenters, six steel workers, six men to maintain the tracks, four riggers, two watchmen, a foreman, and bridge examiner and assistant. The boatmen below always know exactly who's working where and when. "To you and I, the workmen may seem to take awesome risks, balancing on steel tightropes," says Jim Sinclair, a mountaineer himself who thinks nothing of walking up the edge of a box-girder to the top of a cantilever. "But they know what they're doing and the riggers who wire up the mechanised safety cages are highly skilled."
Powered staging was introduced in 1981 and a new cradling system, developed specially for the Forth Bridge—to replace the one condemned under The Health and Safety at Work Act of 1974—has proved successful in trials. In comparison with other sectors of industry, and considering the dangers of working at heights up to 360 feet above the sea, the bridge's safety record is remarkable.
The last fall was in 1970 and the last death was that of Jim Sinclair's predecessor, who was unaccountably dragged along by a train while conducting visitors over the walkway.
The party stops at one of the bridge's four bothy groupings and crosses the track to meet foreman Alex White. Inside, the bothies are equipped with bottled gas for heat, light, hot water and the occasional brew-up—most welcome comforts, particularly in wild weather. But it has to be really rough to stop the work which goes on behind weather-sheeting in gales of up to 40 mph, to general schedules outlined up to five years in advance.
"Sunday is our big day, when fewer trains use the bridge and supplies of goods, including the red oxide of iron paint, are brought out," explains Alex. "People think we paint the bridge from end to end, but, although there is an all-round painting cycle of four years, the supervisors prefer to think in terms of a six-year non-stop programme of painting, cleaning and maintenance."
En route to the Inchgarvie cantilever, past the lights that illuminate the navigational channel below, Jim Sinclair gives the party the all-clear and leads the way down a wooden staircase into the underbelly of the bridge—a world of spans, girders, lattice-work and gang-planks, with the sea ever visible 100 feet below.
It is possible to go down all the way to the caissons and, at this point, to emerge by Inchgarvie Island, forlorn with its abandoned memorials of the past: concrete huts from the last war; the ruins of a fortress erected to protect shipping from pirates in the 15th century; the datum pier from which the early engineers recorded readings of weather, currents and tides; and the circular pile of foundation stones for Bouch's aborted bridge. Here at Inchgarvie, early wayfarers took respite from rough ferry crossings, and the Pictish king Hungus once stopped off to thrust the impaled head of Athelstane into the ground as a warning to others.
Today, a head for heights is required—as well as special indemnity—to climb to the top of one of the cantilevers. Many visitors are content with the superb view from the top of the Jubilee Arch, to which is affixed the plaque commemorating the 1890 opening ceremony by the Prince of Wales.

Right: *In the days of the old steam locos: A revival of interest recently has led to railway preservation societies organising several trips a year across the bridge in this exciting form of transport.*
Left: *One of the 200 trains which, on average, cross the bridge every 24 hours.*

Men at work on the permanent way in 1985.

From here, you can absorb important new features of the landscape: Houndspoint, BP's tanker terminal for the export of North Sea crude, with its hovering launches equipped to deal with the least spillage; the Mossmorran petro-chemical complex, discreetly hiding in the hills near Kirkcaldy; and on the brow of the southern bank, Hewlett-Packard's steadily-expanding Queensferry Division.

On a clear day, the view carries the eye 60 miles west to Ben Lomond above the Loch Ard Forest, where the tributaries of the Forth merge to meander through Flanders Moss to Stirling. From the castle on the rock, the sites of seven historic battlefields—including that of Bannockburn—are graphic testimony to the strategic importance of what was the first fordable point of the Forth until the 19th century. Well in view is the Hawes Inn, from which passenger ferries once plied back and forth, under the soaring arches, to the accompaniment in more recent times of passengers' cameras clicking to capture the balletic dance of steelwork soaring to the sky. With the coming of the Road Bridge, the ferries are no more; but, thanks to the enterprise of a Queensferry man, visitors may still take a trip under the Forth Bridge in the picturesque motor-vessel *Maid of the Forth.*

Throughout the centuries the Queensferry Passage was a majestic, if frequently terrifying crossing. Margaret of England, who became the bride of Malcolm Canmore, is said to have given Queensferry its name after her ship was blown off course to the Scottish coast in 1069 when fleeing the Norman Conquest. Her youngest son, David I, called the crossing *Passagum de Inverkeithin*, and its first mention as the Queen's Ferry is as late as 1164, when Malcolm IV granted the monks of Scone free passage *ad portum reginae*.

Other monarchs who once used the ferry crossing were Alexander I, Alexander III, Robert I, James VI (who gave the Queensferry Passage to Anne of Denmark as a wedding gift in 1589), Charles I, and William of Orange. And the last passengers to use it were royal too—Queen Elizabeth and The Duke of Edinburgh, who made the crossing to North Queensferry before opening the new Forth Road Bridge in 1964.

Walking off the bridge on the south-approach viaduct, the group sees an older workman in fluorescent jacket stooping to pick up a coin. The tradition of throwing coins-for-luck out of carriage windows has faded but not died . . .

"I think it was some old railway worker wanting a holiday in Spain who invented the tradition," says Jim Sinclair with a smile. "We've never seen a £1 coin yet and the 50p pieces surely come from rich Americans."

Queensferry itself provides one of Scotland's prettiest pictures: an attractive huddle of buildings of various eras, shapes and finishes. The Forth Bridge is a listed building, and the village boasts several more buildings of outstanding architectural or historical interest: the Tolbooth, Black Castle, the Carmelite Church, and picturesque dwelling houses built on terraces. Two streets of original Forth Bridge workers' houses still stand at Dalmeny, the village's station. Only one house now belongs to British Rail and its brickwork remains defiantly unpainted in an otherwise thoroughly modernised row. Yet it is a tangible reminder of the human effort that built a superhuman monument to itself . . . to man's determination to conquer the elements and the seemingly impossible.

As the train back to Waverley pulls out, a backward glance is irresistible; as is the conclusion that the Forth Railway Bridge is set to outlive us all—and span at least another century ■

A GRACEFUL NEIGHBOUR: THE FORTH ROAD BRIDGE

Scotsman Photo Library

Two magnificent bridges now span the Forth, to show the world Britain's remarkable mastery of structural engineering, and particularly bridge-building, over the past century; the great Forth Bridge symbolising the Railway Age and its graceful neighbour, the Forth Road Bridge, our own Automobile Age.

Pressure to build a road bridge—which would bring added prosperity to this industrial region of Scotland and open up goods transport and tourism on a much larger scale—began with a proposal in 1923. Three years later, the Ministry of Transport asked a firm of consulting engineers to prepare plans. But a long period of frustration and delay followed . . .

The scheme was shelved during the depression of 1931, revived in 1934 only to be set aside again with the outbreak of World War Two.

It was not until 1957 that the Secretary of State for Scotland granted official permission for the Forth Road Bridge Joint Board to develop the scheme—and it was fitting that the firm of consulting engineers selected was Mott, Hay and Anderson, since one of its founders was rail-bridge designer Sir Benjamin Baker.

The firm took design and the supervision of construction on board in association with Freeman, Fox and Partners.

The superstructure was erected by a consortium known as the ACD Bridge Company, consisting of Sir William Arrol and Company—another link with the railway bridge; the Cleveland Bridge and Engineering Company; and Dorman Long Ltd.

There had been a plan to build a road with a single carriageway above the tracks of the railway bridge at one time, and another to construct a concrete tunnel, both of which were rejected by experts. After an exhaustive investigation of alternative sites—the Forth Bridge already occupied the prime site—the site known as the Mackintosh Rock, half a mile upstream, was selected.

The proposed road bridge would be the first long-span suspension bridge to be built in this country. Its dimensions (main span: 3,300 feet) were comparable to those of the ill-fated Tacoma Narrows suspension bridge in the United States which collapsed spectacularly after only four months of operation in a sudden wind of 42 mph. Though there were no deaths, the incident was a tremendous shock to bridge-builders.

Yet the designers and engineers of the Forth Road Bridge were able to learn a great deal from studying the extensive research which followed the collapse of the American bridge.

An outstanding feature of the Forth Road Bridge is the use of high-tensile steel for the main towers—the overall height of each above its concrete base is 484 feet, the steel extending to 10 feet down into the concrete, giving an overall height to the top of the suspension cables of 492 feet. In one section of each tower there is an electrically-operated lift from deck level to the top of the tower.

The road bridge contains 39,000 tons of steel and took around 300 men three and a half years to construct. It was opened by the Queen on September 4, 1964 ■

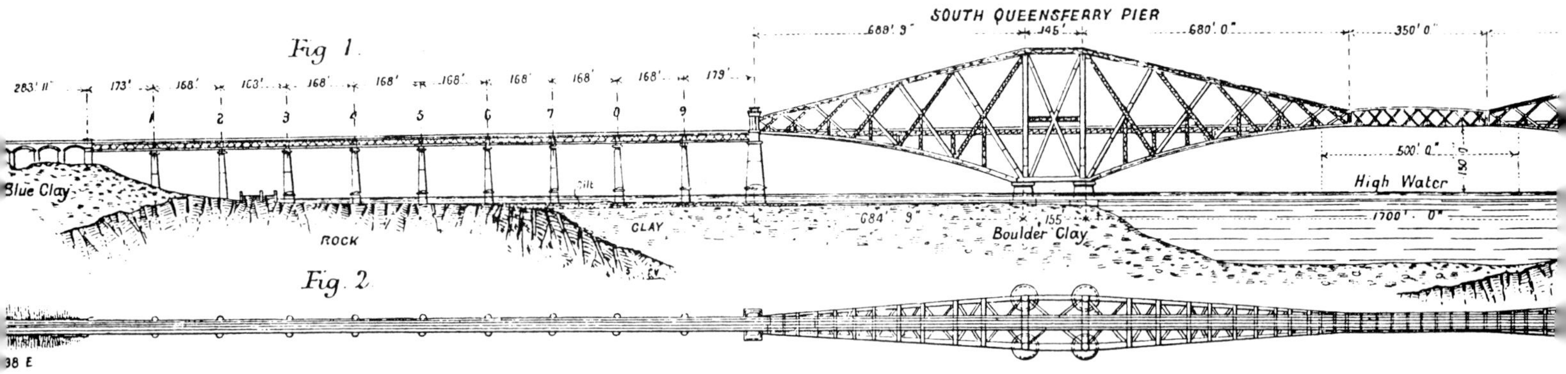

The Forth Bridge is a continuous structure, nearly 1⅝ miles long, soars to 361 feet from high-water mark to the top of the main cantilevers, and cost £3m to construct.

It costs British Rail an average of £750,000 per annum to maintain the bridge.

The bridge is almost one metre longer on a hot summer day than in mid-winter.

Bridge supervisor, Jim Sinclair, routinely inspects the instrument which measures expansion and contraction of the bridge.

The Tracks: Two railway tracks are laid on longitudinal oak timbers fixed inside steel troughs.
The rails are Forth Bridge Section, 56 feet long and weighing 125 lbs per yard and are fastened to the timbers by coach screws. The main expansion joints on the rails are formed by long tongues cut at an angle of 1 in 63, which slide against a backing rail bent at a similar angle. A stepped plate arrangement keeps the running rail always to gauge.

Materials used in construction: 54,000 tons of steel, 194,000 cubic yards of granite, stone and concrete, 21,000 tons of cement and almost 7 million rivets—the last banged into place by the Prince of Wales on March 5, 1890. The rivet is still in the centre of the north suspended girder on the east side of the bridge beside a small plaque commemorating the occasion.

Light during construction: The installation of electric light, a relatively new phenomenon, was one of the first operations of the Forth Bridge Works. Artificial light was needed to allow large numbers of men to work through the night and was a boon to workmen and divers during the sinking of the caissons.

Embarking on a ferry at North Queensferry in 1953.

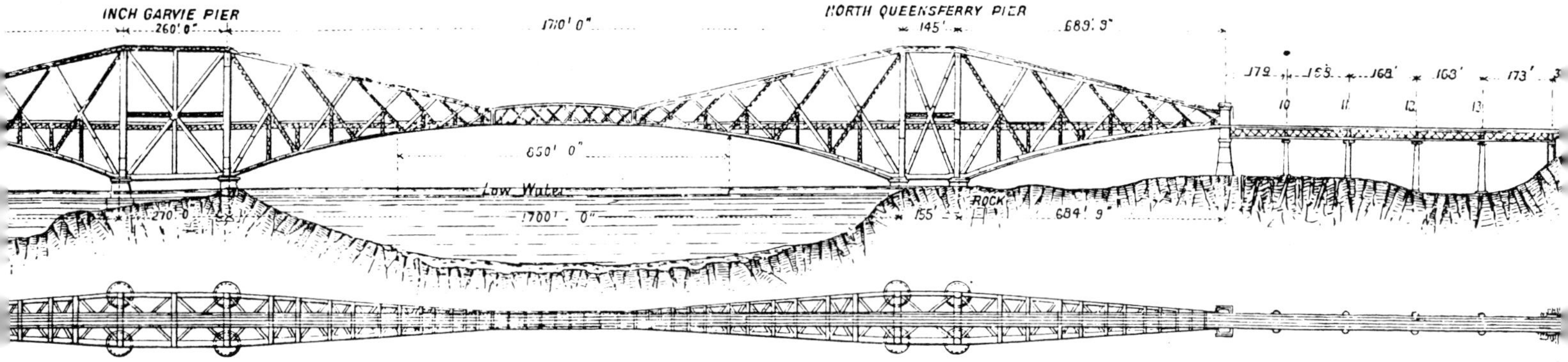

Lucigen oil lights were a 'formidable opponent' to the electric arc. The Wells light was also used on the bridge and during the construction of the Inverkeithing and Aberdour Railways.

Two-thirds of the present work-force live in Queensferry and North Queensferry—as well as several men, now in their 70s, who spent most of their working life on the bridge.

Contrary to popular belief, the Forth Bridge has hardly ever been the chosen location for potential suicides. The road bridge is another matter. It is said that attempts from it are frequent.

Well-defended bridge in World War 2.

Scotsman Photo Library.

Small patches of moss and lichen appear to be the only flora on the bridge, though workmen report having seen rabbits and fieldmice in addition to the numerous sea-birds which use the bridge as a perch—and sometimes attempt to nest high on the cantilevers. A deer once tried to walk across the bridge but was gently turned away.

W. Westhofen, *The Forth Bridge* (London, 1890) remains the authorative account of the bridge's construction.

Rolt Hammond, *The Forth Bridge and its Builders* (London, 1964), which includes a chapter on the building of the Forth Road Bridge is the only modern account of any substance; however, Anthony Murray, *The Forth Railway Bridge: A Celebration* (Edinburgh, 1983) provides a delightful whimsical view, particularly of the bridge's operation after its opening, and reproduces some fascinating examples of bridge memorabilia.

Sir Robert Purvis, *Sir William Arrol: A Memoir* (Edinburgh, 1913) is an enjoyable biography of the bridge's contractor and Hugh Douglas, *Crossing the Forth* (London, 1964) is a most readable general book on the Queensferry Passage.

ONE HUNDRED YEARS AGO

A summary of the construction of the Forth Bridge extracted from the reports to the Board of Trade: 1883-1890

1883
Offices and workshops at Queensferry are erected by June and equipped with machinery by August. Workshops and workmen's cottages also completed at North Queensferry. And at both places, as well as Inchgarvie, landing stages are built by August to enable men and materials to be brought in. Work begins on piers for both north- and south-approach viaducts, including building of cofferdams around the south-side pier-bases which would be under water at high tide. At year's end, caissons for Inchgarvie and North Queensferry are being manufactured on Queensferry beach and arrangements are complete for lighting of whole works.

1884
Queensferry Section: Caisson for south-west pier launched May 26. Both this and the south-east caisson in position by September, north-east caisson launched and north-west floated into position on December 4.
Inchgarvie Section: North-east caisson in position by March and masonry work on this pier completed by year's end. North-west caisson lowered into position in September.
Fife (North Queensferry) Section: Masonry work on north-west and north-east piers complete by March and, on south-west pier, by December.
Average number of men employed in building operation in previous quarter: 1,500 (June); 1,850 (December).

1885
Queensferry: North-west caisson tilts over and sinks on January 1. Recovery operations continue throughout much of year; not refloated until October 19. South-west pier complete by May, south-east by September and north-east shortly afterwards.
Inchgarvie: North-east and north-west piers complete and south-east caisson sunk by May. South-west caisson launched on May 29. Masonry work on south-east pier complete by December.
Fife: Timber staging between main piers to facilitate erection of horizontal tubes begun in May, and tubes in position by September.
Numbers employed: 2,800, including Italians engaged in caissons' compressed-air sinking arrangements (February); 2,200 (September); 2,000 (December).

1886
Queensferry: By August cranes, hoists, winches and riveting machines delivered for erection of vertical columns to support cantilevers. Work on north-west caisson completed February 11. First skewback (south-east) in position by May; the next two (south-west and north-east) by August; and the final one (north-west) by November. Also by then, vertical columns at 116 feet.
Inchgarvie: Tubes between piers in position by March. Skewbacks completed by November.
Fife: All four skewbacks in position by May and vertical columns at 171 feet by November.
Numbers employed: 2,000 (March); 2,180 (May); 2.345 (August); 2,960 (November).

1887
The three vertical columns reach final height and building-out of cantilevers' members begins . . . after which, progress is measured in terms of distance reached by the "branches" from their "trunk".
By November, the whole vertical superstructure above the piers is practically complete and lower members of cantilevers have grown thus—northwards and southwards respectively—at south side: 73 and 60 feet (February); 130 and 122 feet (May); 152 and 126 feet (August); 160 and 152 feet (November). And at Fife side: 130 and 130 feet (May); 130 and 135 feet (August); 152 and 164 feet (November).
Numbers employed: 3,280 (February); 3,410 (May); 3,748 (August); 3,790 (November).

1888
At beginning of year, four double-derrick cranes are delivered which can be moved along the cantilevers' internal viaducts while helping with their construction. Girders therefore begin to be connected in February on Queensferry, Fife and then Inchgarvie sections. As top members of each cantilever reach out and begin to converge with the lower members, they are connected by complex bracing system.
Numbers employed: 3,090 (February); 2,909 (May); 3,270 (August); 3,300 (November).

1889
Masonry work on approach viaducts almost finished by May: south end connected by temporary gangway to cantilever. All three cantilevers practically completed by August and by November central girders of two large spans are connected. All sleepers and rails in place on the south-approach viaduct and most of those on the north. Bridge can now be traversed from end to end.

1890
Bridge underwent final tests on January 20; was opened by HRH the Prince of Wales on March 4.